MOPERS
HOPERS
GROPERS
and
DOPERS

By DR. FREDERICK BAILES

D1526761

Martino Publishing
Mansfield Centre, CT
2014

Martino Publishing
P.O. Box 373,
Mansfield Centre, CT 06250 USA

ISBN   978-1-61427-643-2

© *2014 Martino Publishing*

Cover design by T. Matarazzo

Printed in the United States of America On 100% Acid-Free Paper

MOPERS
HOPERS
GROPERS
and
DOPERS

By DR. FREDERICK BAILES

Mopers — Hopers — Gropers and Dopers

Man faces problems from the moment of his birth. They are a part of life in a universe based upon law. If it were a universe of whim and caprice some could gain freedom from pain and sorrow by wriggling into the good graces of the powers that be. But in a cosmos where every atom is bound in immutable law, and whose principle is order and harmony, problems are merely situations in which one has failed to understand and master the law. The apprentice's insoluble problem is easily solved by the adept journeyman, therefore in one sense there are no problems, only varying levels of understanding, for if the situation can be solved by anyone it ceases to be a problem.

Many persons are ashamed of their difficulties. They mistakenly feel that these are a sign of their depravity or at least of their weakness and hopelessness. Particular sorts of defeat like excessive drinking cause even greater humiliation. The fact is that problems exist as a part of life;

they are the eternal challenge to man's
ingenuity. The only way he can grow is
through opening up the deeper levels and
by enlarging the range of his perceptions.
This is the result of going toward rather
than shrinking from that which is painful
or depressing, meeting it as a condition
and not as a disgrace.

The progress of the race has come about
through skilful and courageous adaptation
to adverse situations as they have presented themselves. Each generation which
faces and solves its own problems extends
the body of knowledge, increases the areas
of man's thinking, and lays a brick in the
walls of man's understanding.

The history of man is similar to the
history of the child. He enters the first
grade with very imperfect knowledge,
and immediately finds himself presented
with problems. These to him are vast,
although to his parents they are small.
He masters them after repeated efforts
and arrives at the end of his first year
with the feeling that he knows much.
Moving into the second grade he finds
himself confronted with entirely new
problems, which in due course he solves.
Through grade after grade he passes,

sometimes thinking that surely there is
nothing more to learn, but finding that
each completion is only the springboard
from which he dives once more into a
beginning.

When he leaves school his education does
not cease. Now the problems are more
diverse. No two individuals have the same
kind, nor do any two individuals react in
the same way to the same set of circumstances. Life thus becomes a challenge.
Never knowing what tomorrow will bring
forth he learns to be adaptable to the
changing conditions of life. But he has
learned one lesson if he has gained anything from school—that no matter how
involved the question seems to be, somewhere there is an answer; no matter how
hopeless the problem, somewhere there is
a solution. Moreover, he has come to as-
sume that man never comes to the end
of his education, never arrives at a place
where there are no more problems.

Man's greatest need is more light. Like
a plant or a tree, he grows only in response to light. Understanding is far
more effective than will power, struggle,
or self-induced force. Once the issues
are clearly seen, the only problem that
remains is that of adjusting oneself to

life in a manner that promotes harmony.
The unhappy truth is that many do not
accomplish this. While many bravely
approach the difficult life situations and
eventually find the key to them, others
turn sour and bitter, or hopeless and dis-
couraged. The latter we call

THE MOPERS

The life tendency of the moper is downward, while the other three classes tend
either slightly or decidedly upward. But
the moper has given up, or has never
got started. Somewhere he has developed
the false idea that the cards are stacked
against him; that the world is in a con-
spiracy to deprive him of his rewards.
He regards himself as the plaything of
a cruel fate, and feels that happiness and
success are a matter of luck or fortune.

He thinks of himself as being different
from others. He magnifies his own experiences, and thinks that they are different from or worse than those of others.
He thinks that no one else has ever suf-
fered as he, no one has ever had to go
through what he goes through. He fails
to see that every situation, painful though
it be, has been met by literally millions
of persons before him. It is unique only

in the fact that it is the first time that
it has happened to him.   His next door
neighbor might at this moment be pass-
ing through something much more devas-
tating, but since he is not whimpering,
the moper does not know that he is cour-
ageously attempting to handle the problem.   If by chance he were to discover
his neighbor's gallant fight, he would prob-
ably decide that it still is not so difficult
as his own.

The moper invariably has a persecution
complex.   This builds up through a series
of steps which are logical, and creeps so
gradually on a person that he is not aware
of it at any stage; in fact, he is often
highly indignant when someone tells him
that this is his real problem.   The complex builds up in the following way: First,
a sense of failure to achieve.   This is
always the first brick in the structure,
failure to react to the deepest urge in human nature, which is the will to win.   This
subconscious urge is woven into the very
fiber of man's nature because generations
of men before him have met and success-
fully faced the intricate problems of living.   There is that in man which feels
that he is made for overcoming, for the
heights, for the possession of joy, health,

prosperity, love, appreciation and respect.
Lacking these, his inner self concedes
failure; it senses the fact that he has been
more in touch with the will to fail than
the will to win—both of which are parts
of his mental inheritance. Man's truest
self yearns to be the expresser of the will
to win; his lesser self desires to express
the will to fail. The self-same law of mind
that produces winning results produces
failure results; success or failure lies within
the man, in the field of his dominant inner
pattern of thought. Consciously one may
wish to win while subconsciously he wills
to fail. Failure to understand this has
caused much despondency among failures,
and bitterness toward the world. Hence
one degenerates into the position of the
moper.

The foregoing usually sounds harsh and
callous to the defeated person. He says,
"Do you think I'm crazy, wanting to fail,
when everything in me cries out for success? Do you think I enjoy financial
stringency, to see my wife having to work,
my children ashamed of their shabby
clothes? Why, I wear my fingers to the
bone, I slave and toil, but I get nowhere.
I tell you, there's no justice in this world.
It doesn't seem to pay to go straight."

The hardest thing in the world to have to say to such a person is that everyone is exactly where he belongs in this world, and that each person gets just what he deserves. It sounds cruel, but it is not. It is merely a statement of fact, based upon the truth which every scientist is trying to tell, that the unchanging law and order of the universe are man's greatest blessings when he cooperates with them, and man's harshest opponents when he fails to co-operate. Since they will not, can not, change their mode of action to coincide with man's ignorance, man must learn to alter his activities to fit them into these unalterable universal principles.

More light is needed. Man must be brought to see that he is always leaning toward one of the two conflicting principles within him, the will to win and the will to fail. His leaning is often entirely unwitting; in fact, he often leans in one direction while wishing and hoping consciously for another. The human mind is often sly, slippery and elusive in its tortuous windings, but it always works according to law; whatever it brings forth is strictly fair. Man gains nothing by railing against it. He who is wise begins to adjust himself and his thinking to 'it.

Seeing the outward form produced by his deeply hidden thought and not liking it, but agreeing that it is eminently fair, he proceeds to use the means for leaning first in the direction of the will to win, then building up his inward thought patterns into the deep expectancy of the flow of the desirable into his affairs. The sick person often has an unwitting desire for his illness, and although it makes him physically miserable, it has compensations in the way of attention and sympathy which in certain tyes of persons outweigh the misery. He will never become well until he leans preponderantly toward the will to win, which in his case is the will to health.

A similar mental operation is necessary in the case of destructive habits. The excessive drinker often says, "I want to quit; I have taken cures and tried everything, but it seems that I am unable to get rid of this habit. What shall I do?"

The fact of the matter is that anyone can quit anything the moment he wants to quit more than he wants to continue. Again this elusive mind tells him that it wants to quit, but that impulse is only in the surface layers of his thought. It must penetrate deeper until it occupies the whole man. Secretly he is leaning toward the will to fail, either because it is an escape from reality into fantasy or because he is not entirely willing to give up some faintly lingering pleasure connected with his drinking. He has not yet marshalled all the reasons, organized all the motives that will swing his larger self over to the will to win. Sometimes it takes a tragic experience such as a terrible automobile wreck in which someone is killed to bring together at one time all the necessary ingredients for complete decision. Whatever it is, when all of himself decides to quit there will be no struggle; the habit will fall away from him.

His consciousness of failure to line up with his larger self quite naturally leads into a sense of guilt. This in turn leads into either a spoken or unspoken self-condemnation. Since he condemns himself, it is logical that he expects others to condemn him; therefore he is on the defensive with others, expecting their censure. Since he does not see where he is wrong, but feels that he is the victim of circumstances instead of a plain, straight working of mental law, he begins to think others are "picking on him"; that they don't understand his terrific struggle. This leads inevitably into self-pity, which

is the forerunner of the persecution idea.
Without noticing it, he first feels that the
universe is persecuting him, then unwit-
tingly he begins to persecute himself,
then he feels that others persecute him.
This may or may not develop into a full-
fledged persecution complex, but at any
rate he becomes a moper.

The person in whom more light shines
is not unduly cast down when others hurt
his feelings. He knows that ruthlessness
is rather common in human nature; only
a child thinks differently. The moper
has to learn that no matter what the
world does it cannot hurt him; only he
has the power to hurt himself.

One of the plaints of the moper is that
there is no opportunity any more. Men
like Edison and Kettering have said that
never in the world's history have there
been so many opportunities as in the pres-
ent day. The moper has to learn that
opportunities do not always come labelled
as such—often they come in the guise of
disaster. The literature of biography is
crowded with stellar names who would
never have amounted to anything except
for severe physical handicaps, or a brutal-
ly poverty stricken childhood environment.
To the blind man the sun does not shine,

the flowers have no beauty. Man must get his eyes open to the fact that when one is born his opportunity is born with him. It circles above him all his life. But it never intrudes—it awaits his recognition of it. Man's great need is for more light; he must get his eyes open to opportunity.

There is some one thing that each person can do better than anyone else in the world, if he can find it. This may sound strange but it is true. No one else has ever stepped into the world with exactly the same combination of gifts, slants, tendencies, strengths and weaknesses. Even to his fingerprints, each person is different from anyone else.

This unique inheritance means that while others may surpass him in certain spheres there is some place where his unique make-up makes him superior to all others. Few men are successful at all points. Many have failed at several things before finding their peculiar niche. But there is a place, and the seeking soul usually finds it, if he keeps his expectancy high. The moper has given up. The world is not against him—he is against himself. His negative attitude renders him blind to his opportunity.

A man sat in a huge auditorium listen-
ing to Dr. Russell Conwell deliver his
famous lecture on man's inner resources,
entitled "Acres of Diamonds." As the
lecture proceeded, he grew more and more
dispirited. Everything had gone wrong
for him all his life, it seemed. It was
easy for the speaker, financially successful, to talk as though opportunity lay on
every hand. Let him get the bad breaks
this moper had had, and he'd change his
tune. As he sat with hands cupped in
his lap, a hairpin fell out of the hair of
the woman in front of him. In those
days hairpins were not crinkled. He
looked at it, then fell again into his mood
of despondency. Unthinkingly he bent
the pin, a little here and a little there.
Finally he put it in his pocket and went
home. His wife found the pin and asked
the usual questions. Satisfied that he was
telling the truth, she placed it in her hair
and went about her housework. To her
surprise it stayed in while the ordinary,
smooth hairpins fell out repeatedly. She
got an idea, had the crinkled pin patented,
and they became rich. The unhappy moper had not recognized opportunity even
when it was dropped into his hands.

Thousands of persons passed beneath
the huge chandelier in St. Peter's, but to

them it was a menace. Seeing this weighty object sway gently to and fro, they hurried past, lest in falling it crush them. But to Michelangelo it was opportunity. He stood watching it, and thinking deep thoughts. Inner light dawned, and from the hazardous chandelier he worked out the principle of the pendulum.

Many men have been hit by falling apples; their response has been annoyance at having their siesta disturbed. But to Isaac Newton it was opportunity. "Why do falling objects always fall downward, not upward?" Thus Newton discovered the principle of gravitation, which served science well until Einstein.

For centuries men pulled their shirts on over their heads. They cussed at the garment that mussed their hair, but did nothing about it. But one man said, "Why shouldn't we wear shirts like coats?" He made the new type shirt, and it made him a fortune.

From time immemorial men shaved with the straight blade razor, and cut themselves repeatedly. But no one did anything about it until one man said, "I believe I can figure out a guard for that blade." The safety razor made him a multi-millionaire.

The head of the United States patent office resigned in the middle of the last century because he said: "So many things have been invented that there is no field for invention any longer, and my job will soon be obsolete." His mental descendants in the great family of mopers are still saying the same thing, while barely literate immigrants arriving in the land of opportunity with little but their courage are soon busy inventing gadgets which the world is eager to buy, and becoming presidents of our large manufacturing enterprises. The world is alive and shrieking with opportunity, but as long as one remains a moper, he might just as well be living in darkest Africa.

THE HOPERS

The hoper is a much more desirable individual, for his tendency is upward. It is said of the great Michelangelo that he spent so much time standing on cathedral floors studying the masterpieces of art on wall and dome that his neck became permanently fixed, so that in later years he came to be known as "the man with the upward look." The hoper might not yet have achieved great things, but at least he is a man with an upward look;

the chances are that he will eventually arrive at a much higher standard of living.

The stages toward attainment might be set down somewhat as follows: one is made conscious of the possibility of higher levels of life. His initial response is usually the skeptical "Well, it MIGHT be so, but I doubt it." From this he goes on to the next stage, "I HOPE it's so." Then, "I BELIEVE it could be so." Eventually he proves it to himself, when he is able to say, "I KNOW it's so." Hoping is an essential stage in proving and knowing, while moping is an effective barrier to proof.

There are two kinds of hopers, those who dream, and those who do something about their dreams. The entire advance of civilization has been due to humanity's practical dreamers who added performance to vision. On the other hand millions of visionaries have dreamed dreams and have become immersed in the dream, never translating it into action. This is a world of action; men of action are needed. The fatuous smile of the theoretical hoper becomes a grinning death mask behind which lie rich dreams which were allowed to die of malnutrition. The classi-

cal example of the theoretical hoper was
Charles Dickens' character, Mr. Micawber.
Dickens knew the character well, for it
was his own father. This cheerful gent
was like the lilies of the field which toil
not, neither do they spin.. He was always
"waiting for something to turn up," even
though it became necessary to pawn the
silver and furniture piece by piece while
waiting. Finally he was cast into Mar-
shalsea Debtors' Prison, and languished
there still waiting for "something to turn
up." What matter if his family were in
dire want, with the half starved children
slaving in the factory.

Dickens grew up with the memory of
this optimistic poverty, and wanted none
of it. He knew that while it is inspiring
to have one's head in the clouds, it is
much more comfortable to keep one's feet
on the ground at the same time. Vision
and action are the twin elements of successful living. Dickens dreamed greater
dreams than his father had done, but he
coupled them with action. He had higher
hopes than his father had had, but he
backed them up with performance.
The world is full of those who wish,
dream and drift. Desire is a lusty giant
within them, but decisive action is a puny
infant. They see others happily achieving

the good things; they look with wistful eyes toward the heights steadily reached by those whom they imagine to be more fortunate. They see those more daring souls sending their ships across the world and reaping the reward; they, too, wait for their ships to come in. The only trouble is that they have never sent their ships out. Vision and action are the two oars that row the boat. One is not enough. Vision without action is visionary; action without vision is drudgery.

It is imperative that one act as soon as possible on any constructive vision, because the fine glow of fervor that surrounds it is likely to evaporate with postponement, and it is not always easy to recapture an inspiring picture once lost.

It is a mistake to think of success as something one gets. It is something that he is. When we talk of the elements of success we are not discussing ways and means, rules and practices; we are discussing the character, ideals and approach to life of the person. Man is a composite of all he thinks. His business or personal success is merely a projection of himself. Successful lives are built by successful men. Something invisible has first occurred within themselves; that which becomes visible is only the shadow thrown

by the reality. The so-called lucky person is not lucky. Even in those extremely
rare instances where it seems almost certain that the success is undeserved it will
be found that he carries a mental "horse-
shoe in his hip pocket." Something hidden away within him has drawn the good
fortune.

The person who refuses to accept
mediocrity will in some way rise above it.
Man is constantly being presented with
a best and a second best. It is easy to be
contented with the latter. The next pre-
sentation will naturally be on a lower
scale; therefore the second best becomes
progressively lower. Scientific animal
breeders mate the best of their herds in
order to improve the breed; then take the
best offspring and mate them again. To
mate the lesser is progressively to deterio-
rate the strain. There is a tendency to-
day in the social, economic and industrial
world to level down to the less efficient
rather than constantly trying to level up
to the most efficient or the average. It
is one of the dangers to a society which
has climbed to the peak of industrial performance as the United States has done.
One keen observer has said that modern
democracy's most egregious blunder has
been the cult of "the superior rights of

the inferior individual." The isolated instances in which he is helped may be necessary and valuable, but when it becomes a tricky political policy, persisted in and steadily fostered, it can lead nowhere but to individual progressive deterioration and eventually to the disintegration of the society which fosters it.

GROPERS

The groper is a persistently hopeful creature, whose tendency is decidedly upward. He is sincere and willing but often confused. He may or may not feel sorry for himself from time to time, but at least he attempts to do something about it. The less desirable class of gropers easily become habitual "tasters," but never go on to completely digest any one philosophy of life. They drift from lecture to lecture, take up one "ism" after another, never synthesizing the various points of view to produce a philosophy of their own.

They drift from numerology into astrology; from this they move over into "the occult," then dabble in spiritualism. They are enthusiastic Freudians for a time; then are agog over "color therapy."

Later they are successively students of Science of Mind, and Christian Science, with periodic dips into Unity, using the phraseology of all these systems interchangeably and in a completely befuddled manner. They are psychoanalyzed, vocationally tested, personality tested, but they still are unable to make life a successful, satisfying experience. They are gropers to no useful purpose, playing with their little spades and buckets on the edge of the ocean, but never getting in and learning to swim.

We are not saying anything derogatory of these various systems just mentioned. Each of them has a core of truth which, if followed persistently, would be of great assistance to the groper. But we must deplore the aimless drifting of those whose groping never brings them to a settled conviction that "This is it." It is quite probable that each one of us has groped his way around many or all of these systems before finally arriving at our destination, for only by such groping can one arrive at a spiritual philosophy that satisfies him. It is not the search, but the dilly-dallying that is destructive of deep conviction. It matters not how many "ologies" one examines before he ultimately arrives at a destination. The chief thing is not the search but the arrival. The habitual "taster" seldom arrives.

Most thinking persons have felt that there must be an answer to the great problems of man's existence, but the practical person wants something workable. He is intolerant of fine-spun theories that look well on paper. He needs and must have something that will produce definite results in his health problem, his business and financial situation, his domestic and personality difficulties, in his mastery over destructive habits, and particularly in his inward sense of oneness with the Infinite. It must be reasonable, logical, yet spiritual in order to satisfy all sides of his life. Finally he is willing to incorporate it into his thought life and his daily affairs as a working principal. This type of groper has always led himself and others onto the higher levels of living, for he combines vision with action.

Man is a searching being. He has not advanced his civilization through startling jumps, but by painfully groping his way along the walls of his environment. The old saying that he who seeks shall find has always been true; therefore the groper who maintains the persistently hopeful attitude will eventually make his way into the final class, the dopers.

DOPERS

This class of people was named dopers in order to carry out the alliterative sequence; it may be a misnomer, for it does not refer to moronic individuals as it would appear at first sight. The word is used in a slangy sense to describe those who have the 'right dope" on life. It is the highest class of all, and the life tendency is decidedly upward. Whereas the groper is sincere and willing but confused, the doper has come to the place where he knows where he is going, and has a rather clear idea of the way to get there. While the extreme type of groper never settles, and drifts from teacher to teacher without ever taking root anywhere, the doper has found that he advances much more rapidly when he stays with one teacher who is clear and decisive. Thus he is saved from the confusion of apparently contradictory teaching. The word contradictory is used advisedly because the vital principle of all progress is essentially the same, but the different terminology used in different circles often confuses the student, who is thus kept in the groping stage.

The "doper" is marked by a certain decisiveness which grows out of an assurance that he knows the principles through which he can attain his desires. He has come to know that while an individual may experience defeat in his life, life itself is undefeatable. He therefore surrenders himself to the flow of the invincible life in him, and acts as though he has every right to succeed.

But successful living is more specific than this. Man's mental world is governed by mental law just as certainly as his physical world operates through physical law. Happy living is no more a matter of chance than is successful chemistry. The laws of both chemistry and happiness are man's master until he comes to understand them; when he understands them they become his servants. The ingredients of satisfaction lie everywhere at man's hand, waiting for him to organize them. To go into them completely would be impossible in this short booklet; they are covered more extensively in other books listed at the end of this one. But they can be given here in sufficient outline to start one on the way into the land of his desires.

The first thing to know is that man always controls his circumstances; they never control him. Man is not a body

containing a mind, but a mind inhabiting
and controlling a body. As such he is
eternal, and the eternal always dominates
the temporal.

The second thing to remember is that
man controls his moods; his fears and
doubts are merely thought-forms which
he has created; they do not come of their
own accord. He can re-form them to suit
his view of life, and they have no choice
but to obey him. The moper has sur-
rendered to the idea that his moods gov-
ern him and that there is nothing he can
do about it. The doper has learned that
the only power his moods have is that
which he yields up to them, and he has
determined to surrender no more. When-
ever he finds himself giving utterance to
negative ideas, he checks them as soon as
possible, and endeavors not to repeat
them. Gradually he comes to a position
of self mastery through practice.

Moreover, he knows that the predomi-
nant character of his thought is indicated
by the kinds of things upon which his
mind most readily dwells. If he finds
himself occupied overmuch with the ideas
of defeat, unfairness and hopelessness,
this establishes his dominant inner pat-

tern of thought and thus stamps his character. A person's character is the aggregate of his thought.

Thought is not something that can be held within the confines of a physical cranium. It is an energy which flows from him in waves. Therefore, everyone carries with him an atmosphere of defeat or victory, illness or health, poverty or prosperity, which can be sensed by sensitive persons in spite of the false appearance often put on to cover it up.

This mental atmosphere operates as a principle of attraction. Man is momentarily attracting to himself that which is like his thought. Therefore the bulk of his outer experiences are similar to the preponderance of his inner thought. There is no mystery about it—it is a law of his being. The outward experience level and the inward thought level are exactly equal. One often says that he wishes he could attract certain specific forms of good, but concludes with the deadening utterance, "But I never attract anything." Man is always attracting something. What he means is that he never attracts the rich and fine and healthy. The law of attraction works unceasingly within his affairs. It is coupled with another law which de-

termines how much of anything he will
attract. Some persons approach life in
so hopeless a manner that even when
some good drops into their lives they cannot believe it, and they are sure that such
good fortune cannot last. Therefore, they
shut their good away from them, and it
does not last. The doper is he who has
learned to expect big things and who
makes preparation for big things.

Another side of the great law of mind
is that of circulation, sometimes called
giving and receiving. Receiving is merely
giving on its return trip. He whose whole
purpose in life is to get will find himself
sadly disappointed. Strange though it
may seem, man gets by giving. Business
men have found that "service" and courte-
sy, which in themselves have no cash
value, are highly important in building
a business. To many this sounds like
hypocrisy when uttered by a business man,
but it is fast becoming a fixed business
principle. The doper cultivates an inner
generosity of spirit, in which criticism of
others is replaced by kindly understanding, resentment by friendliness, and past
defeats and losses are tossed aside by a
new philosophical attitude of, "So what?"

If he has been penurious with his family, he begins to "loosen up" without plunging into a wild orgy of extravagance. His contributions to his church are materially increased; he keeps an eye open for opportunities to help others less fortunate than he; he is generous in his estimation of the motives of others, and warm in his praise and encouragement. These may seem to be small things, yet it is the small things which affect our destinies and change the course of our lives. He goes toward people instead of retreating from them, and if he has been so lacking in worldly goods that he cannot give money to others, he gives his warmest, most genuine smile. It is the change of attitude that counts more than the express form it takes. Cheerfulness costs nothing and can be practiced on Skid Row as well as in a mansion. A smile can light up the face of the unemployed as well as that of the rich. It has well been said, "A merry heart doeth good like medicine." It has been the beginning of the healing of hurt souls, hurt businesses and hurt pocketbooks. But it won't work unless one works it.

"But that is easier said than done." If that is the reaction, he had better go back to his moper's hill and sit amid the ashes

with Job, for he lacks the necessary character to be happy even if his circumstances
were changed by a fairy wand. The happiness of the doper is so much above the
misery of the moper that it is worth any
effort, especially when that effort will
assuredly be rewarded by the joy of life
that wins. In fact, he will find himself
occupying the mourner's seat without
Job, because that wise man finally saw
that life was not against him, that God
was not cursing him, and a changed attitude brought him twice what he had
before. The ancient patriarch passed
through the four stages from moper to
doper and has lived for the encouragement of men for three thousand years.

This book is the substance of a lecture delivered by the author Sunday morning, November 28, 1948, in the Ritz Theatre, 5214 Wilshire Boulevard, Los Angeles, California.

———————